THAT WOULD EXPLAIN THE VIOLINIST

THAT WOULD EXPLAIN THE VIOLINIST

Sunil Freeman

GUT PUNCH PRESS
Cabin John, Maryland

Some of the poems in this book have appeared, sometimes in slightly different versions, in the following publications:

Abbey: "November 11, 1989," "Outcast in an Irish Bar." *The Federal Poet*: "She's Got an Unbroken String of Broken Hearts." *Gargoyle*: "Thirty, Feeling Like Seventeen Again." *Anniversary Issue* featuring Heatherstone Poets & New Voices (Heatherstone Press): "After the Divorce," "Thinking of James Wright, Alexandria, Virginia." *Lip Service*: "Land's End, San Francisco," "'Loon,' Algonquin Park, c. 1960." "Moonrise, Nags Head, N.C.," "Poverty," "Sunday Morning," "Tracking Beethoven's Tenth." *Metropolitain*: "Almost Aboriginal," "Bethesda Metro Stop," Trinity Amplified." *RaiZirr*: "After Returning to Suburban Maryland, I Visit Montgomery Mall." *Samisdat*: "Just Say No." *Sulphur River Literary Review*: "Pierce Street Annex." *WPFW 89.3 FM Poetry Anthology*: "Second Floor Dance Studio"

Some of the poems in this book have appeared, with poems by Jim Henley and Michael Schaffner, in *Men Without Drums — The Book* (Autoexec.Press), a limited edition chapbook.

First Edition

Library of Congress
Cataloging in Publication No.: 92-72280

ISBN: 0-945144-03-2

Cover art: "Sequentia" (detail)
bamboo stick and ink by Eva Santorini

Gut Punch Press
PO Box 105
Cabin John, MD 20818

Production by Richard Peabody

Typeset at The Writer's Center
Bethesda, Maryland

For family and other friends,
and for all those who have influenced me
and those who should have.

Some of you know who you are,
some of you don't,
and I don't even know
who some of you are.

Contents

Eric Dolphy Lives!

The Georgetown Cafe

1.

We all leave our old selves at the door
whenever we climb the few steps off
chic Wisconsin Avenue and enter
something like a truckstop greasy spoon
run by Arabs. There's a jukebox
and a Pac-Man machine, a menu
with western omelettes, steak and cheese
subs, filafels and babaghanouj. A balding
Arab rises from his cluster of friends
to adjust the tv for Saturday afternoon
college football. The back of his head
shows a crescent hairline. He fiddles
at the controls, angles the screen
toward the group, and then they ignore it
together, so the game might be
a background of ouds, the thrum
of some distant bazaar. Suddenly
they're drawn in, stoked on coffee, hands
fluttering like Islamic birds. The referee
has made a stupid call, so they argue
back in Arabic. I don't need subtitles;
their hands are calligraphy in motion.

2.

I hold my coffee cup with both hands.
My first time here was with a Georgetown
student approaching graduation
after the bars had closed. "Come to California
with me," she said. Our hands locked,
fingers laced as if to approximate Islamic art,
palms slow dancing. A couple's cigarette smoke
floated cues I couldn't quite decipher.
We had entered the world of gypsy violins,

the place where black and white movies are born.
That was another decade, another life.
Now, as then, time thickens here into something
like honey, a hint of rosewater and saffron.
Two blond undergrads, Georgetown University
written all over them, flirt with a bunch
of young Arab guys. A Christian woman
in her forties argues religion
with a Moslem man who might be twenty-two.
They're friendly and feisty as Methodist
and Baptist neighbors in the Old South.
An elderly regular settles in at the counter
and mock growls at a young man,
"So, are you the chef today?"
"Yes." He's so proud I guess
he began washing dishes. "Compliments
to the chef," I tell the waiter
as I leave. I smile, waiting in cold rain
for a bus, and the happiness
won't let go of me.

Georgetown Waterfront, Saturday Afternoon, July 1990

The canvas shrugs itself awake with scores of us
scattered across the landscape inside. A memory
of breeze, a mild shudder and a Rip Van Winkle stretch
as we come, yawning, alive. The river's sheet
music without lines. Boats laze on the nonchalant flow.

If perfection is everywhere why move at all?
Across the channel on the island, maples, poplars,
willows and more venture a study in green which rises
into textural frenzy, Rousseau foliage.
Kudzu avalanches over the trees.

Jets trace sonic arcs, music from another dimension.
Bicyclists wheel over planks, their percussive rolls
a muffled bass marimba — a punctuation of sorts,
but I can't clue together the choreography,
grammar, frequency.
                                        I'd rather track the progress
of four Euro jet set women amused by something. Laughter,
breasts, blondes, brunettes. Tremors ripple
the waterfront in their wake as male radars lock in.

A large boat churns upriver, one of the men
on board pointing toward the shore,
where architecture rises, symmetrical,
fountain spray framed like a computer's half-
remembered dream. A street person offers hits
off his bottle of evian water to select passersby.
He's friends with the universe, he says.
He sees the ten million dollar hand pointing
from the river and waves back a cheerful "Yo!"
bottle raised. Sparrows land at my feet
and cock their heads as if to ask,
"Don't you know you are Francis of Assisi?"

Sunday Morning

White ceiling, blue walls.
A skewed rectangle of light
frames swaying shadows of plants.
Shade scuttles across darker shadow,
light on brighter light.

Prisms scatter colors that flicker,
swell and blink out percussive figures
till I hear something somewhere
between wind chimes and silence.
A car hums past; its light eases across the room.

We'll get up, drink smoky trails
toward morning (Darjeeling? Lapsang Souchong?);
lean back into silence, a language of molecules
where a speck of floating dust
is an epic, a star.

Meskerem, Vegetable Mesob

(For Julia)

Eyes hawklike, hands quivering
with intelligence. I've never had dinner
with a woman who was on *It's Academic*,
or never knew it. It's like a game board,
how we contemplate these mounds
on this injera circle. I go for leafy greens
in the center. You reach to my right,
orange goop that tastes almost like meat.

You tell of the kale in Kenya
called *sukuma wiki* in Swahili, "push week,"
because when the migration started to Nairobi,
and working people went hungry, they ate it to push
through to the end of the work week. *Sukuma wiki.*
Our waitress overhears. Her eyes sharpen;
her whole body comes to attention.
I dream of dating an Ethiopian woman.

We trade disastrous date stories — my friend
who got a senior cheerleader to say yes
when he was a junior, then convinced his dad
to let him have the Continental convertible.
This was maybe 1966. He knew he'd arrived:
her mom and dad smiled in the front yard;
beside them, an Aqua Velva ad come alive,
their daughter of so many high school dreams.
He palmed the wheel into the driveway
with his right hand, waved with his left,
casual, perfect suburban Tai Chi.
The brakes failed and he crashed in the garage.

Lights glow — a golden hum, a murmur;
my one beer feels like it could be three.
We harvest these vegetable mounds till we're down

to patterns on a spongy canvas —
an edible 2-D technicolor Stonehenge, sort of.
Each splotch might be a story,
but we get the check; you work out the tip,
stumbling briefly on the math. I'm no help —
this is too delicious, watching a woman who was
on *It's Academic* wrestling with percentages.

Almost Aboriginal

(Metrobus, August Sun)

1.

An old Chinese man, mouth dropped open,
cradled by lull and hum, basks
like an iguana. His head snaps back;

he surfaces fast through layers
of pressure ribbed tight at the temples.
What pictures, emeralds on velvet, fade?

China before Mao? California in the '20s?
His eyes unglaze. He seizes the cord,
rings for the next stop, sways

with the weight of two grocery bags,
balances, shuffles to the door
and tells the driver "thank you" so gently.

2.

Eyes half open, tuned close
to their own lashes.
I'm a mad Busby Berkeley watching

prismed egg-shaped colors dance
to the rise and fall of my eyelids;
iridescent butterfly-winged signs

on the road to the dream time,
where spectrum and spectral are one.
Telephone wires dip,

then rise to the next bar,
like a blues guitarist bending a note
up, up, till it taps in every heart.

December, 20 Degrees, Night Bus to Montgomery Mall

Scientists think they're God,
mixing the chromes, playing
with the poly bonds and all.

I like my DNA just fine,
thank you very much.

My name's Eve. I'm thirty-five,
so they couldn't do the reverse
spiral on my genes. Damn
corkscrew sons of bitches.

Hate to think of the next
generations. Roll the dice
for five billion people
when they know absolutely
zero. Less than snake eyes.
Bunch of crap.

My name's Eve. Last name's Smith.
My grandma's a Smith, too. Tell me
about it. I can tell you a thing
or two about cows' eyes. Bullshit.

What time do you have?
I've been on a midnight train.
I've marched. Sure, man.
They didn't crack your poly bonds.
It's a war. Hell, you know
what I'm talking about.

The doctors are all assholes,
most of them anyway. Sometimes
you realize half your life's twisted
to fit other peoples' careers.
Crazy if you ask me.

Poverty

(for Daisy, and for Smoky, 1974-1985)

1.

Some nights Daisy catches you coming home and talks
two hours, a gnarled rasp, slow and steady,
rooted seven decades into West Virginia.
You're working 60 to 80 hour weeks, itching for food,
a tall glass of Jameson and Elvis Costello.
You wait for the pause to break away, but it never
comes. You joke to your roommate about her
yogic breathing skills — she can talk all day
without taking a breath. But you smile and lean
on one foot, then the other, on the landing
in your Arlington garden apartments.

> Her husband cussed her out forty years,
> then keeled over dead, but her son picked up
> where he left off. He never hits her.
> She has Jesus, her cat Smoky and knitting
> for grandchildren who don't trust love
> if it doesn't look like something on TV.
> Still she knits but the arthritis is catching up.
>
> *And my Grandma had arthritis*
> *so bad she'd get her eyebrows*
> *all tight to catch the pain*
> *and that was before*
> *we hit the potholes.*

You escape two hours later, gulp the whiskey
so you're primal before *Imperial Bedroom*
hits the turntable. Costello hisses: "History . . ."
The S's cut like whips. At ten she knocks;

this might be a heart attack. Early in the morning
you both cab back. She's okay for now.

2.

You move. A year later you bump into her
at a used bookstore. She had to move last month;
the new apartment didn't take cats. Her voice
takes you back to the stunted trees on Spruce Knob
that survive without your pity, then silence as she strokes
the bookstore's cat, hand tracing the curve near the ear.
You see the girl seventy years ago, tears itching
and tickling after a spanking.
All you can hear is the purr.

Capitol Hill, Washington, D.C.

I bring out the mother in old Jewish women,
so when the sun went down at the corner store
she shook her head and said, "Go home."

Nights, white noise turns dark;
it takes shapes I can't quite make out.
Sirens, shouts. Wisps of fur pricked static
on every neck. People die most every night.
It's all in walking distance.

Last week I went to the Outer Banks.
Wind and surf moaned a sound
you might hear if you looked too long
at a Francis Bacon painting.
I half-heard shouts from a redneck bar
just beyond earshot. A car cruised
the beach road.

What the Man in the Frayed Sweater Might Be Thinking

(Metrobus, February)

His eyes shift like he's tracking reflections
so I look at the motion picture mirrored
in the glass. Translucent buses and cars
run down ghost pedestrians who keep on
walking; a cartoon world. He stares out
the window as an armada of cumulus clouds
races across the sky. Riffles of cirrus
might be ripples on a wind-tossed lake.
Lamp posts, grayish-white, suggest sycamores.
The window reflects rectangular chunks of sky
like some old avant-garde photograph.

The man's in his late thirties.
Watching him is like seeing pictures
of European Jews before *Kristallnacht*.
He's alive for now; the way he turns
his head, I'm pretty sure he's noticed
the whine by the left back wheel
sounds like a Middle Eastern translation
of the blues. Miles Davis could have polished it
into something unforgettable.

When his eyes close I think of waiting
for buses — how the cold hammers a man
to a place where warmth, when it arrives
barreling down the road, triggers a drone
which begins in bone marrow and spreads
till his temples are those of a child,
and when that buzz synchronizes
with the hum of the bus he closes his eyes,
alive and not hurting, and that's enough.

Outcast in an Irish Bar

1.

He sputters across the room like an alien
with a glitch in the "walk" software,
full of tentatives, hesitations.
It's not medical, not the booze.
He was born with a tattoo on his forehead: Outcast.

He studies the happiness that swirls around him.
Men and women smile like they do in ads.
Tapping hands and feet, metronomes sloshing
through deep seas of Guinness; heads bob
like dolls on dashboards.

He hugs the melody like a talisman
that will take him back to kindergarten
and erase that tattoo.

2.

Last call; only the music
lovers remain. He twitches,
grasps his leg with his left hand,
gulps and walks to the fiddler.

The words come out like he's driving
his boss's BMW on sheet ice:
"A slow air would be nice."

The fiddler is a legend —
say his name in the right bars in Dublin,
and you're family.

He cradles the ancient air
as if it were baby Jesus.

The hush glows as everyone goes
to some hidden place on private blue highways.
The music ends. His eyes open
as he rides the lonesome road back.
The fiddler looks just to him and smiles.

Southern Madonna with Arab Children

(After the Sigmar Polke Exhibit at the Hirshhorn)

A distant siren blends, seamless,
onto the merry-go-round's crankshaft
melody, like the echoey shimmer
that rides Philip Glass' highbrow
calliope tunes. Four dark-eyed children,

part Arab, spin circles around
a thirtyish brunette. They angle
closer, smiling, arms tilted,
then arc back out, a solar system
of little Sufis. The oldest might be seven.
The woman calls them in a Southern accent

that turns heads, and gravity outpulls
her children's centrifugal force.
They fall into line for the ride.
Doves improvise jazzy arcs,
long looped serene stretches
like visual anthems, Coltrane's *Crescent*.

I cross the mall, the carousel
muffled as if by an unthreaded quilt
of sounds — runners on loose rock, buses,
sirens. The wind sounds like a hotshot
guitarist going to town with a wah-wah pedal;
it ricochets Doppler pyrotechnics.

I turn to see the carousel. Traffic
has sealed its melodies; it twirls,
silent fragment spun out of a dream —
Southern Madonna and Arab children
on horseback in the wind, pulled taut
between gravity and the centrifuge.

For My Grandfather

After the serious part we went downstairs,
as you'd planned it, and told Lem Freeman stories,
recalled your ninety-nine years,
warmed ourselves before embers of that flame
which burst from the backwoods of South Carolina.
It was a great roast; you'd have loved it.

Liberal Southern Baptist preacher, professor
and fiddler, who pondered reincarnation
and Darwin, held interracial study groups
in your North Carolina home in the 1940s,
and faithfully tuned your radio to Jesse Helms,
'cause he was so dumb it was funny.

This whole crazy family is a thundering echo of you.
I once suspected I was your favorite grandchild
but now I think a few of us hoped we were —
and that's the way it should be.

Moonrise, Nags Head, N.C.

We watch from the porch,
a budding family (first baby asleep inside)
and assorted friends, selected,
as friends will be selected,
like a greatest hits album.

Rocking chairs echo the waves;
beer ("brewed in the shadow of Kilimanjaro"),
cold and bitter on the tongue,
warm and sweet in the brain.
Fish swim in the dark;
they don't smell tomorrow's Chardonnay.

Conversation grows to hold
lengthening patches of silence.
Perhaps being God would be like being
the eye behind the camera,
watching folks like us on a night like this.

How many conceptions here over 65 years?
On the beach, on a full moon like tonight?
How many nights have parents
said penumbra — rosy lips
on the nipple of the moon — to a child?

Someone says dunes are essentially waves.
Imagine riding a brake pedal
long as the Outer Banks —
a surge of whitecaps rerun in sand
green-capped by dune grasses.

We laugh about getting older —
our twenties slipped away
in a slow motion riptide.
We brought a VCR, not a radio,
and agree: "Hope we get old before we die."

Bethesda Metro Stop, 1987

Science fiction creeps up on me.
One day I catch myself
looking at a tree sculpture —
holograms on circular metallic leaves —
and realize I'm already lost in the future.

The holograms catch light and roll it
around the spectrum as I ride the escalator.
Turquoise, silver, lavender, gold —
Crayola royalty sharpened to a high sheen.
I remember the happiness long ago
in each bright orange nickel popsicle,

eat an 80-cent chocolate chip cookie
and watch buildings slash the sky
into punk haircuts. I remind myself
it's just atoms, the dance of Shiva.
(An old god can teach us new tricks.)

Mescaline, 1971

The senses are primed to jitterbug
with the things of the senses so I turn

off the lights, crawl into bed,
burrow under a quilt, bring my knees up,
fetal, and close my eyes.

Time forgets to spin itself out.
Nothing but colors and sounds

and something important, maybe my soul,
flowing in and out of a tooth
(three left of the left incisor)
like solar flares.

Sounds and dot patterns spin fugues
that shoot from the center of that tooth,
then zoom back into my mouth.

I'm in outer space. There's something
attached to my foot. Oh!
It's the earth.

Just Say No

The public awareness clip cuts
through sales pitches that imply
you have a volcano in your pants
and a Nerf ball in your skull.

She's 15 or 16, cute but vulnerable,
and she's talking right to you:

> I started with limericks.
> It was fun. It was daring.
> After a while I was playing
> with rhymes all the time.
> Then my friend Billy
> told me about free verse.
>
> Billy's dead.

The camera closes in on her eyes.
They're tunnels to hell.
Mercifully, a voice-over breaks in.
It's a doctor on a prime time series;
a voice we all trust:

> Sylvia Plath. Suicide.
> John Berryman. Suicide.
> Ezra Pound. Insanity.
> Dylan Thomas. Suicide by alcohol.
>
> Billy. Suicide.
> When will it end?

The Guitarist, After the Band Breaks Up

1. Thirty-fourth Birthday

Wave or particle? Mist droplets pop
on skin like microscopic chips of wind.
Dogwoods, poplars, sidewalk and street,
stripped the lacquer of sunshine,
glow tranquil as ancient Japan,
or April in Bethesda.

He's on a Metrobus when the sky unzips itself,
a drumroll thrashing pavement like a video
of keypunched computer paper,
drops big and white as pearls;
rain so hard only a smile could protect you.
He's cocooned in the bus, head humming,
like a teenager on the brink of epiphany.

2. Seventeen

Sligo Creek Park,
sky dark through layers
of leaves, feathery, fern-like
scrims upon scrims,

airiness packed atop itself
till it's reverse pressure —
there should be something
deep above the jet black,

above the fertile canopy,
woodsmell, earth.
And then it clicks —
the stars.

It's only the hashish
blowing through

his wide-eyed mind,
but he doesn't know that yet

so he smiles like a baby
reaching for a mirror,
touching it. Bugs glow,
green on the forest floor.

3. Back in Bethesda, Metro Center Plaza, Outdoors

Watercolor grays unfold into pyramids of light.
Cumulus clouds across blue sky so fast he slips
into a time-lapse feel, eyes holding the eastward flight;
this will be the weather map on tonight's local news.

The picture flattens

> (Kids on skateboards.
> Trees tracing every nuance of wind.
> Silvery sheen of bird chatter —
> jazz-tinged mobile of call and response.
> Eric Dolphy Lives! A couple,
> dreamy-eyed as a coffee ad in Paris.)

into a simple march of clouds across land.

He holds a mouthful of coffee
like a slow drag, lets it pluck
each tastebud till he feels
the caffeine rise into his brain
as the coffee goes down.
He slouches into his chair
and watches a daydream coalesce.

Again, the early '70s: Baltimore.
Paper airplanes flying to the distant stage
between sets at a Mahavishnu Orchestra concert.
One at a time, so the entire crowd —

maybe two thousand — focused on each plane
as it caught an updraft, went farther than expected,
finally touched down. A collective sigh, surrender,
release, over and over,

till the loud webs exploded —
call it jazz-rock, call it electronic Indian music.
He can't remember if any airplanes reached the stage;
the fogging of memory seems just right —
undefined emerald promises that grew
into this afternoon where he sits till night,
its huge bear hug.

Nightmare, 'Round Midnight

Her tonearm eyes
my Monk album
like a Doberman
looking over a kitten.

As it bears
into the groove
it grinds down
the long spiralling

line of memory:
this album in early college,
magnolias full bloom
sweet late nights

I crossed campus
to my girlfriend's dorm,
life lush as
a never ending wet dream.

But that was then.
Her arms and legs
spread to cover
the bed like kudzu;

she smiles,
bares her teeth,
turns
and climbs on top.

The Preacher's Son and the Tornado

The sky's a dark, lumpy mattress; then
he sees the original serpent corkscrewed
into a drill in the hands of a God gone
Old Testament — no quarter, no surrender.

The preacher's son is just out of college.
A splinter from his heart squirts up
into a drop of spit. Two decades
distill into two gulps for air:

> The day in sixth grade he proved
> himself with the class toughs.
> They caught crayfish and burned them
> in gasoline, threw the flaming, half-alive,
> clawing husks on two third graders.
>
> Nights, rock 'n' roll
> down low on the car radio,
> perfume like a close memory
> of honeysuckle patches beside asphalt
> so moist he could almost feel it breathe,
> and Mary Ellen, the girl who let him
> go all the way. Later, alone,
> he prayed himself to sleep.

Tonight he'll fall back into himself
but now his heart is only *Jesus, Jesus, Jesus*
as he watches and waits for the sound
of a thousand freight trains.

Tracking Beethoven's Tenth

What became of the pre-sound heroic emotions
reaching — like God to Adam in Sistine Chapel —
to become anthem, the barely awakened motifs,
the pianissimo sighs of possibility,
the pinpoint slivers of silence,
all lining up like a hundred airplanes
in holding patterns before that arcing descent
from thin air to thought to note to ink to paper
— the air traffic control nightmare
that finally sings: "Symphony."

A squadron without landing gear,
a gong, reigning spectral, seeking a mallet.

An air conditioner's cool "Om"
hums every album in the *Schwann Catalog*, and more.

Invisible Segues

Sundial

Watch the day float by,
subtle and mysterious
as a fretless bass.

Trinity Amplified

We are our heartbeats,
but bass drum and bass press
loud new thumps into our chests till we grow
to hold two, three hearts. The guitar solos,

big as the sun. The keyboard man
thrashes his artificial ivories
but no sounds attach to his mime.
The sax player strums reggae-

flavored air guitar across the bell of his tenor.
Lights change chords in another language.
Colors play musical chairs on the drum set.
Green icicle mike stands, red coronas of cymbals,

gold drums. They shift — green coronas,
then all green, smoke thickening the beams
till the band is inside a huge cartoon
of an artichoke. The beat pushes our ribs;

we're released into the huge single cell
we have become webbed and bound
in a glue of volume.
The artichoke segues

into red, purple, orange. A ray
fat up the middle. The guitarist leans
into it, graceful as Ted Williams.
A gold line drive; a clean, hard shot of blues.

The Brickskellar

(for Suzanne, John and Christy)

What *was* the Rolling Stones song
in that old movie? Christy, Southern blonde
with a grey and white cat named Jeb Stuart,
an accent to match, clicks her fingers
to summon titles. *Gimme Shelter? Brown Sugar?*
Suzanne smiles, deep in the center of a buzz.
Oldies and beer. We order a third
or fourth round. *Get Off My Cloud?*
The last drops of Sierra Nevada Porter fall
on a deep head like rain on snow.
Our hunger for simile is "like,
encoded into our genes."

Rings of Guinness foam stack on a half-full glass.
They look like four or five fish,
tails rising, parallel angles on ice
behind the counter at a corner market
or mountain ridges rolling to the horizon.
Weren't fish fossils found in mountains?
Everything connects if you look easily enough.
Imagine a Japanese heavy metal band
called the Bruise Brothers.
19th Nervous Breakdown? Stray Cat Blues?
Whitewater one moment, our stream of thoughts
pools into silence like cresting a hill
on Skyline Drive, the valley suddenly golden.
It's October.
                    Recently I've been hearing
a gorgeous slow reggae take
on *Magic Carpet Ride* in my head.
Let the sound take you away.

CBS 25 Years Later

In '61 or '62 *My Weekly Reader* promised
the future — SSTs, outer space.
1969 was my edge of possibility;
1970 was science fiction.
The '80s, so distant they'd never come,
were the perfectly chinked wall
that held in the universe.

Tonight, pictures from Dallas,
Washington footage. I remember
grief wrapped tight as a cocoon
that bitter morning.

But a year later my neighbor
Steve and I played in the backyard:
I'd announce, "Mickey Mantle,"
toss up the ball and slug it
to left field. Fly balls past him
that reached the rock garden were home runs.

We could almost taste the cotton candy,
the hotdogs, happy as kids
who didn't yet know the trajectory
had ripped a line harsher than San Andreas.

Good people went to heaven.
Sometimes I saw him in dreams;
I told him we missed him.

November 11, 1989

The champagne flows from the same wellspring
that makes people dance like gods
at the wall. It floods our screens,
too large for one city,

one country or two,
until the pictures from Berlin translate
into sky over Bethesda.
Two couples, right out of *Esquire* and *Vogue*,

freeze. They stare at the sunset, randomly
next to an old man who's barely blue collar,
not yet on the street.
All five watch together, silent:

Orange slathered, smeared thick,
a snapshot out of focus; glacial bleed
of melting sherbet blending ever sharper
to the north into sawtoothed orange peaks

till photorealism meets a big looped arc of blue
so deep it recalls memories I might have had
before I knew what memory was.
The blue, a bay overhead. Coves and fjords

pierce its slow curve of coastline.
Telephone wires suggest a musical staff melted
like Dali's clocks. I almost hear psalms.
Strangers, we glide like inhabitants

of our happiest songs. Orange light
right down to the sidewalk.
I breathe it. Church bells chime;
a tuning fork hums in my chest.

Composition for Piano and Rapidly Exiting Yuppies

(For Cecil Taylor)

Geometric chunks dance a space blues
inside a jackhammer strobe of sound.

Two runs chant back, forth,
back again, like a field holler
two centuries later, been to college,
come from the city.

A motif spins itself
into a Mobius Strip.

Languid three second chords
like clouds in a Caribbean paradise
nestled into a hurricane —
distilled, compacted time.

You're cooking; the yuppies rush
out like irrelevant steam,
leaving us, the crazy-eyed people.
We're family. When the lights rise
we'll become mirrors,
hundreds of crazy-eyed mirrors.

Lord, I love that communion.

Second Floor Dance Studio

Aquamarine and white squares
ruled off by silver bars
gone to gray; what might have been
Mondrian fades into something
Hopper could understand.

In another universe
the stars on the sign
might twinkle neon stardust;
here they look like asterisks.

I see the dancers and know
there must be music. They waltz,
perhaps so deep in Strauss
it could be Hershey's Syrup.

They twirl to the window
like goldfish rising
to catch light and grace it
with one muscular moment.
Beige curtains frame the picture;
they might be lily pads.

Old Angler's Inn, Lunch Outdoors

An old toy: Eggs in eggs in eggs:
Pattycake Pattycake and Crayola landscapes
sleep in him as he dreams in you.
You do glow as eight months of life
grow toward visible light,
swell that veil of flesh.

A bee floats parabolas
around some purple flowers,
cuts quicksilver currents of breeze.
Leaves show soft undersides,
a thousand fluttering eyelids.
Butter just melts.

I slice white chocolate mousse cake
so silky I know how good it will be,
so pause, empty fork midair,
to savor that tactile moment
before taste buds blossom.

We blend into the picture,
stroll the canal, watch the river,
wander off trail among tiny blue flowers,
huge jack-in-the-pulpits,
reflect on layers of reflection,

chocolate mousse cake
to the souls of Escher and Monet.
Sunshine on reflected light,
shadow on tree on sky in water
and vice versa.

A lone goose reminds me
of years ago, alone here:
the wake of one goose

echoes the "V" of geese in flight.
Greedy geese swim to us, two by two;
you wonder if they really mate for life.

Maybe. It's never a duet (or trio)
though, but a double concerto.
You're both building one
worthy of Brahms, and I,
a second violin, share this
promiscuous light.

"Loon," Algonquin Park, c. 1960

Silver birch shimmered
so crisp in that Ontario
light, sight couldn't hold
it all; so something
like hands on the temples,

a murmur as all that
overflow shine eased
almost into sound,
like chimes, but soft;
air tuned so high
it hinted at maple syrup.

The first blackberry
was a surprise, its globed
facets gemlike; then
we found a new universe
in our mouths. We ate
like gods by the dirt road.

I grew fluid in the lake's
and rowboat's slow lapping.
Not enough air pressure
to speak of a wind;
it reached me halfway,
I could just feel my skin.

My father said, "loon,"
after the bird's cry.
His voice pulled me
to attention and I heard
his word hook to the call.

I gave in to that weaving:

words, sounds that cover
the sounds of the world.

We packed the gray Fairlane
when the time came. I held
three syllables, the box
my parents never knew
they gave me to hold it all,

and replayed the sound
in my head as we drove home.
Sometimes it was dark wood
or a jewelled case in the sun:
Algonquin. Algonquin. Algonquin.

Pierce Street Annex

Susan, former flower child
(California, vintage Summer of Love),
polarized against herself —

Yanged when she should have Yinned.
Now she's upwardly mobile
in spite of her best intentions.

After work party in a singles bar.
Strange synthesizer stuff, jockeying
into the fast lane; a few shakes

of avant-garde sprinkled
into a bubbling corporate stew.
She scans the crowd, smiles,

far away, an anthropologist
from Venus. "Jimmy Mack" spins on.
They dance. She's home.

Land's End, San Francisco

(for Aileen)

We lean into the wind,
watch fragments of rainbow
blink when waves hit cliffs;
an offbeat rhythm.

We'd reach for each other,
perhaps; it's been
ten years. But we don't
recall that movement.
So our eyes go gentle —
a current, a drowsy
trace of rainbow.

Sky so crisp the crystal's
on the tip of my tongue.
Light jackets
after sunset; last night

we could have been
kids on a jet:
the city a fairy tale
of diamonds scattered
across the bay far below
our road into Berkeley.

Was it yesterday we ate
chocolate ice cream
at the corner
of Haight and Ashbury,
or the day before?

Tobago, January 1981

Coconut groves, empty beaches,
and now, Bird of Paradise Island offshore
to our right. We're almost slow motion
on the road to Charlotteville,
a cratered, winding cross

between Zen riddles and "Que sera, sera"
that turns our watches into mandalas that
kaleidoscope into happy faces, eyes closed,
and purr like cats in meditative trance.

The land rises, patient bread.
We inch down from the eventual crest,
a carful, to houses that bask, pearls
in the sun. An old hippie stands by a VW van,
his smile rooted into his whole body —
his face, his stance — organic as a mango tree.

We descend to a bay wide as the grin of God
on a good day. At night, breezes
roll in like breakers over a sea
of sun-baked warmth; lights hum
secret lullabies to the shore.

Cicadas, Twilight

God's maracas, tiniest staccato ticks
piled so thick they go all curvy,
backwash and cross rhythms

till it's white noise that keeps
coming on. They all speak one tongue
(or leg twitch) I suppose, but together

it's Babel. I let the dizziness come
over me, then my ears mosey around
in the spin until they find hints:

tremors here, fault lines there;
they insinuate shapes in the warp
and weave. The street man

squints and stops and turns
then spins fast to glimpse
the dance in all that rattle.

He cackles at the sky; I don't
shy away. I've heard the shapes;
if they could all line up

just right — not quite diamonds,
poly-somethings — I'd coax them,
like zippers, and pull.

Alone at the Bar

The background buzz splinters
into cubist sounds. Angles everywhere,
but none quite right. Glasses hang
like angelic bats behind the bar;
their reflections glisten
parabolas, white and silver,
that might be blueprints,
clues, so close I can almost touch.

The hard stuff rises on triple tiers
to play light like a pipe organ;
nozzles pointing to heaven might be
an exhibit of amputated hookahs.

Wild Turkey next to Bushmills so I recall
my father, who heard Brendan on a fast reel,
then said, "He sounds like your grandfather."
Irish reels, backwoods Appalachian fiddle music.
The bottles, touching, could be posing
at a family reunion. I search for the right
slant of ricocheted light to hear
the high harmonies in that smoky brilliance,
that sweet fire. Time coasts into a vacuum.

Single Malt Scotch

She sets her cup of Earl Grey by the IBM,
mildly watches it steam, looks out the window
of her study. Maybe a highland Scotch
for a change — some peat, some fire.
She imagines the glass, the casual elegant

motion to her lips. Laphroaig? Macallan?
She likes the picture just right, not too much.
Perhaps she should have an affair. It isn't
raining, but it might as well be. She recalls
Venice and Greek islands. Thinking of her husband

she finds the Montblanc and pens:
"And you and I? Ennui." She scratches it out
and exhales a charcoal sigh that obscures
Venice, the islands, the blinking
green cursor, garish as a grin.

She admires the bookshelves; their smell
holds her, almost an embrace.

After the Divorce

One afternoon, on a long run, he's drawn
to the river. He's surprised by a woman
in lotus position at the old outcropping.
She turns slowly, as if she expected him,
and he thinks, "If this were 1970
this would be an omen."
She looks like his wife twenty years ago.

He recalls a day with her at this same place,
the river saturated with light.
What was it she said?
"Stillness borne on moving waters."
They understood something then.

He scans the bridge's arcs;
he never knew math could be so beautiful.
Percussive architectural chatter
rises above distant cars and buses.
Silvery surfaces spray light
back to the sky. The landscape is capped
by a storybook blue — he suddenly remembers
elephants in cars, red balls, hedgehogs
in toadstool bungalows at forest's edge.
He smiles to the woman and leaves.

Her stillness follows him, an echo
of a haiku, a sandalwood memory, into town.
The street is an Indian bazaar,
silence under thick swatches of sounds
like canvas implicit in a painting.
So it all becomes a painting,
molten gold drawing his eye to the bank dome.

He imagines fall, some woman he doesn't yet know
raising her glass to catch evening light.

"We've all been wounded," she doesn't say,
her eyes generous. He'll accept her hand, let her
trace lines as if to draft a treaty on his palm.

On the waterfront, boats, sunbathers, daydreamers.
The river is a symphony for deaf people.
Light floats, not quite on silence — something more
like a tambura's narcotic drone, netting everything.

After Moving Back to Suburban Maryland, I Visit Montgomery Mall

(Late October, 1988)

Malls are a language I've forgotten.
The big stores anchor the color-coded key,
cardinal, like winds on ancient maps.
I can't find the "You are Here" arrow.

A toddler has just discovered free will
but can't decide what to do with it.
He stands, paralyzed with options.
His smile freezes, curls into bewilderment.
Mom grips the empty baby carriage;
dad struggles not to peek at his watch.
They look to each other, a tired love,
as if they see for the first time
the slippery slope to middle age.

A store with framed Ansel Adams posters —
Moon and Half Dome, Moonrise, Hernandez.
(How many people, alive in those houses
when he snapped the shutter,
are now in his foreground, the graveyard?)
Did they meet on the other side?
Blind alleys, dead ends —

maybe there is no "You are Here" arrow.
I half expect the Minotaur, rakish,
the right accessories, earth tones
(if they're still in) or black. Whatever.
Musk to drive the virgins wild; they're strewn
about his inner suite like a casting call
for a perfume ad — Obsession, or Opium, or maybe
that new one, Fuck My Brains Out.

(Its post-contemporary offspring,
Fuck! My Brain's Out!)

He casts a knowing glance — virgins my ass! —
at the tilts of their eyebrows, their lipstick, blush.
The mascara. He always meant to explore
the mythic roots of mascara.
Nipples everywhere like a feast
of giant goosebumps. He glides into action.
They don't invite me in. I circle back

to tables with high school kids handing out leaflets
on drug abuse. Images move to coalesce
so I approach for literature.

Kids so red white and blue looking you'd think
the sixties were scrubbed away
with some New Improved Lysol.
They shrink from me. (These suburban adventures
highlight the trace of John Brown in my eyes.)
I retreat; we glare at each other.
I don't hate them; I love how big our species is.
Whitman said, "I am large, I contain multitudes."
Together, we contradict each other; we are large.

Outside, a tree rides slow ripples of earth
like another idea of an aircraft carrier;
its leaves gold-orange, monarch butterflies,
antennae reading the wind, about to fly.

She's Got an Unbroken String of Broken Hearts

If she travelled in different circles
she'd inspire a dozen
Country and Western classics
before reaching thirty.

We lean toward the last embers
before they go down
like the sun.

She speaks of the others
that didn't work out.
I sympathize with those men,
and all who will follow.

Her voice is a drug.
The chill, far away,
touches my skin.

Later, I hear a line from the refrain,
pain shot like a syringe
of uncut emotion straight
to the singer's heart.
A steel guitar cries,
a crippled wolf abandoned by the pack.

Dream Girl

She belongs in a Beach
Boys' song; blonde
who automatically bestows
nobility on her beau.

The bar breathes,
full-throttle tidal
roar of Saturday night.

I try to ease past
the lace and chiffon
of her prom-queen persona
but never touch the bedrock
of personality.

Vacuous beauty: Bud
Lite in Waterford.

Everywhere, snippets
of coherence layered
like geology gone berserk
in a sea of vocals.
(You say "Babel"
I say "babble.")

The jukebox plays
"Send in the Clowns"
three hours too soon.

I'm Fred Astaire,
tap dancing on a
spotlit stage of quicksand.

Thirty, Feeling Like Seventeen Again

"Time present and time past
Are both perhaps present in time future,
And time future contained in time past."
— T.S. Eliot

Sunlight slowly claims your living room, a minimalist
choreography Pythagoras would admire. I push
up from the sofa to wash the last dishes as you give in
to my "pretty please with maple syrup on top"
and stretch for the paper to count me the hyphens
in the punk critic's latest review. A cluster:

"Ten, eleven, twelve," voice rising with the count;
your laughter soprano above the faucet's hum.
"I'm not yet half through. Twenty."
Gasps upon groans as you reach

"the ornamental baroque excesses of the neo-post-
punk-country-folk-psychedelic revivalists" —
or something like that. (And I thought
I wasn't yet middle aged.)

Your cat clings to a thin outcropping of shadow
under the piano. He watches me like the waiters
in your favorite bar: I'm your current love.

Weekends, our mornings stretch a seamless horizon
to afternoon, beyond. Nothing wrong with this
picture: pancakes, a noncommittal cat,
a midwestern woman. Dishes done, I return,

hoping Eliot was right (when were we?), kiss
to pierce your veil of giggles ("twenty-six,
twenty-seven, twenty-eight. Damn,
you made me lose count.")

Thinking of James Wright, Alexandria, Virginia

The ceiling fan might as well be on Qualuudes,
but it's just right in this second floor bar
of dark wood, old anchors and exposed brick.
The second slow cold Bass tames the heat
into a vague memory of morphine, so the pickup
Irish band wails tunes in a room gone goofy,
suffused with slow motion grace. The fiddler,
grown bold on his third beer, bullshits up a storm.
So the giants got tired of fighting and went
to the corner pub and partied for days . . . .
Say, is this a bar?
                                        I think O'Carolan would like
his tunes sent out on this air, centuries later,
where a young girl stares, still,
as if in the presence of Jesus, or Big Bird.
She's with her parents and older sister.
One day she might write of climbing old wooden stairs
to a room lazy with friendly heat, where hands, feet
and legs fluttered to fiddles, guitar, flutes and pipes;
how she looked out and saw leaves riding the breeze
and the room slowly filled with people who heard music
drifting to the street. Perhaps her poem
will have the words *anchors, fiddles, stroll.* Watching
the girl absorbing the room like a perfect disciple,

I picture the almost cellular osmosis
on slow capillary streets; from ice cream cone
to book store to coffee shop to gallery to reels
to crabcakes. Afternoons where we all freefloat,
given over to some larger dream, perhaps
to join a small crowd, feet tapping, that sways
into the sweet pain as a man blows
blues harp above a woman's walking bassline
on the street and all of Old Town
might be a hammock in Minnesota, a hawk overhead.
We are living our lives.

This Would Explain the Title

Because I was a vocal proponent of this volume's title, Sunil asked that I write a brief afterword explaining why this book is called what it is, and not, for example, *Invisible Segues*, which it nearly was called and which is, perhaps, a less cryptic description of how Sunil's poems work and move than *That Would Explain the Violinist*. I voted for the latter title, however, for reasons of both circumstance and content. I'll explain the circumstance first.

For eight consecutive Tuesday nights in the fall of 1991, a group of us would meet after Writer's Center classes ended and go out for a very late dinner. Sunil was working at the Center on those nights; Rick Peabody, Paula Buck and I were teaching classes; Derrick Hsu would join us after closing up the Old Forest Book Shop; Gretchen Sinclair, the only non-writer in the group, would come along, I think, because she knew how much we needed someone who didn't always speak in metaphor. We would wait in the front room of the Center for the last workshop participants to trickle out so Sunil could lock up.

On one of those nights, Sunil noticed Robert "Sparky" Spates loitering outside, violin case in hand. I now know that Sparky plays with a number of local ensembles and duos, including *The Pheromones*, and that Jimmy Pheromone of said duo was taking Joanna Biggar's workshop, which also met at the Center on Tuesday nights. At the time this incident occured, however, only a couple of us knew who Sparky was and only Sunil knew that his sometime collaborator was lurking upstairs.

So Sunil — with the kind of audible clicking that the hard drive produces when you turn on your computer — looked at Sparky, remembered Jimmy, and burst out with, "That would explain the violinist!" None of us knew what he was talking about, and by the time he realized that an explanation was in order, we had all concocted much more interesting theories around our friend's non sequitur.

O.K., so maybe you had to be there. But what brings this anecdote out of the realm of the in-joke and into the realm of the appropriate title is, I think, that it provides a kind of metaphor for the way Sunil's poems manifest themselves. As I read through this collection, I feel a channel of thought — that clicking hard drive again — running beneath the pages. The poems dip into that channel and pull up fragments — dialogue, song lyrics, characters, bars — that once assembled, achieve wholeness from line to line, from poem to poem.

In that way, this book is very much like the landscape in which so much of it lives. As Sunil's poems navigate the territory in and around D.C., they take on some of the eccentric, fractured beauty of this place. And that, I think, explains this collection's melancholy weather, the people, the sounds, the streets and the violinist.

— Rose Solari

Biography

All things considered, "Sunil Freeman" isn't that unusual a name. His parents met at the refugee camp in Kurukshetra, India, in 1947. His father, from North Carolina, was a Quaker volunteer; his mother, from Uttar Pradesh, was a volunteer in charge of the camp's pre-school program. Evenings, she taught Hindi to adults.

He has lived most of his life in the Washington, D.C. metropolitan area, except for a few years in India, North Carolina and Pennsylvania. He has a degree in journalism from the University of Maryland, and he works at The Writer's Center in Bethesda, where, among other things, he is managing editor of *Poet Lore*.